Borderless Broads:

New Adventures for the Midlife Woman

Get Yourself an Outrageously Innovative, Hugely Satisfying, Remarkable Life

Morgana Morgaine

Morgana Morgaine

Asheville, North Carolina

Morgana@MorganaMorgaine.com

www.MorganaMorgaine.com

www.HumorIsHealthy.com

ISBN: 978-0-615-51943-2

Morgana Morgaine offers:

- **Training workshops for women in midlife seeking to live a more collective lifestyle**, what she calls "pod living." She advocates lifestyle choices that offer the right balance of supportive structure and individual sovereignty to nurture women who seek to deepen spiritually, to explode into creative expression, and to thrive!

  Her workshops invite women to consider "Beguine-thinking," taking a journey back to 13th-century Europe to be inspired by a group of women who successfully lived and worked in creative collectives. (E-mail her at Morgana@MorganaMorgaine.com.)

- **Keynotes and workshops** on "Living Your Life through the Lens of Laughter" and "Turning Working Professionals into Healthy Humorists, One Red Nose at a Time!" **Laughter and Play are essential elements for living a "higher octave" life.** These events are offered to any human eager to enjoy the "art of play"! (See www.HumorIsHealthy.com for more information.)

- **Her e-book, "Turn Depression into Expression, 5 Ways to *Move* You."** DOWNLOAD the book from www.MorganaMorgaine.com. **Depression of any kind stops you in your tracks and prevents you from living life full out**! It is an epidemic these days.

- **Individual and group coaching** for individuals interested in repurposing their life's journey for inner peace and outer success! (See www.MorganaMorgaine.com for more information.)

Borderless Broads is dedicated to
women everywhere who understand that
"There comes a time when everyone must make an act of power in order to proceed." (Lynne Andrews)

This book is "my act of power".

I eagerly await yours...

Acknowledgements

A Deep Bow to:

- My Coach and Soul friend, Joy Letsinger
- My "What do you think of this?", Collaborator and Friend, Ann Bohan
- My very supportive British Borderless Broad, Christine Davies (say that 10x at warp speed!)
- My Canadian Cheerleader, Bethany Eaton
- My Everlasting Friend, Linda Hortter
- Beverley Ann Grant Lipscomb, Australian Aboriginal woman of the Wiradjuri Nation NSW, for permission to use her image, "Coming Home" (2007), on the book cover.
- And many-a-friend who cheered me on!

Who Is Morgana Morgaine?

Morgana Morgaine, born in Denver, Colorado, grew "suitcases for feet" early on and lived here, there, and abroad. Her work has followed an equally checkered path. She has been a nurse anesthetist, putting people to sleep, and a therapist and coach, waking people up!

She has been a **trainer of clowns**, mostly everyday folks wanting to spread delight in the world. She continues to give keynotes on "Turning Working Professionals into Healthy Humorists, One Red Nose at a Time!" and offers workshops on Laughter and Play. (See www.HumorisHealthy.com.)

She is a **life coach, mentor, and way-shower** for those eager to make their inner and outer lives more their own—freedom seekers! She embraces soul as the reason for our existence, echoing Plato's belief that "the purpose of life is the tendance of the soul." Through writing, teaching, and coaching, she inspires those desiring to live a higher octave life. (See www.MorganaMorgaine.com.)

Morgana **conducts workshops for women** looking for a new adventure in midlife. She is a passionate advocate for "pod living," shared-living designs with the right mix of supportive structure and independence to encourage women to deepen spiritually, expand their creative expression, and thrive!

She currently calls Asheville, North Carolina, and Santa Fe, New Mexico, home; she is always on the lookout, however, for new habitats and new people with whom to play—**a true borderless broad**!

"When a writer writes from the heart of what matters to him (her) personally, the writing is often both personal and powerful. ...Part of our duty as writers is to do the work of honestly determining what matters to us and to write about that"

—Julia Cameron, *The Artist's Way Every Day*

CONTENTS

Introduction

"I would not want all my words
To parade around this world
In pretty costumes,

So, I will tell you something
Of the barroom view of love.

Love is grabbing hold of the great lion's mane
And wrestling and rolling deep into existence
While the beloved gets rough
And begins to maul you alive."

—Hafiz

This book is written to you, one midlife woman to another, for the sole purpose of inspiring you: to *grab hold of your life like the great lion's mane and wrestle and roll deeper* into **your existence**.

To embrace this third destiny time, age 50 and beyond, as **a new spiritual frontier,** to be lived consciously and with new mind guided by your deep feminine instincts.

To commit yourself to living by wisdom that works and **breaking patterns** in your life that don't work.

To entertain the idea that much of what you have chosen as the blueprint for your life may no longer fit, and now, in midlife, it is time to become **a radical shape-**

shifter; one who is willing to let go of thoughts, beliefs, and structures that have defined you in favor of fresh vital ones for **who you are becoming NOW.**

Each segment of this book has a "MAKE IT YOUR OWN" section where I encourage you to take what I have written, reflect on it, and **shape it to fit you.**

Allow yourself to get messy and "mind-less" with it. Be honest. Be willing to throw out what you need to throw out. Expand and radiate.

Because...

It is for the adventure of it. It is for choosing to live life full out!

"Come to the cliff, [she] said.
No, we are afraid.
Come to the cliff, [she] said.
They came. [She] pushed them
And they flew"

—Stuart Wilde

Prologue: Midlife—*Magic is Afoot*

I remember that the first 40-plus years of my life were defined pretty much by my relationship with an alarm clock to get me going, a job of someone else's making to keep me in money, and a social group to give some cohesiveness to it all—not an atypical Western cultural blueprint for living.

Then around 50ish, I seemed to have a DNA-encoded moment that flipped a switch. I began to have the yearning to be more deliberate in my life, more awake, and, for sure, more choosy about what I believed, what I wanted, and most of all, how I felt as I walked through the moments of my day.

The next years were spent largely questioning and dissolving much of the early "training" that came with family and schooling and living in the culture of my birth. During this time, I left a relationship, moved from West to East and changed my career path with an intermediary step teaching the "art of clowning" to adults; a great metaphor for watching my life increasingly "lighten up."

I have now put it all together, the snippets of wisdom that work, the ways of seeing that keep me lighter, moving, and dedicated to living life full out, as best I can. Keeping in mind, however, that change is a constant and I will have many more periods of "putting it all together" as I shape-shift yet again and again.

And now on to you; the reader.

I am utterly convinced that midlife is the most pregnant time in your life. You have the track record of having walked this planet for some years and having negotiated your way. You may have been biologically pregnant as part of your biography or not, but now you are filled with the eggs of a different kind of creativity, a creativity that comes from making choices and decisions based on who you really are and NOT simply as a result of your social training. It may be all new terrain for you, or you may have been in a midlife shift for some time.

No matter, either way it is an adventure. I am offering inspiration for the shift: quotes, stories, ideas, and challenges to your thinking. **Magic is truly afoot** for you, my egg- laying midlife wonder!

Use this book as your own personal boot camp, envisioning just how you would like your next 50-plus years to unfold, as your soul would have it!

"At 50,
She left her spiritual adolescence
Behind her;
Found the purpose of her life,
Scope of her gifts,
And an outlet
For her creative energies"

—Deirdre Green, *The Gold in the Crucible:*
Theresa of Avila and the Western Mystical Tradition

Midlife Is a Striptease

"I'm going through my life like a cellar and throwing out everything that's dirty or doesn't fit, the false smiles, forged history and obscene scrawls. It's hard work, but I'm singing in my labor and I can hear you and all women singing with me."

—Anonymous

"Let it go. Let it go. Let it ALL go!"—So say the soothsayers of midlife.

We enter a new zone around age 50, more or less, where the years of eggs and biology that might have been a primary focus are over. Work may very well remain a huge part of our lives, but something is different. The difference is that parts of our lives begin to drop away of their own accord. It might be breakups in relationships, or deaths, or career endings. Whatever it is, we begin to detect a different scent in the air, the scent of change. Our choice now is to participate full out in designing what we want or allow circumstances to take us where they will.

Our most compelling purpose at this time of life is to sift through the debris and break lifelong patterns we inherited by virtue of being part of the human lineage. This is a perfect and pivotal time to embrace experimentation, adventure, and the art of doing it differently as we seek a deeper, more meaningful personal purpose.

This is where you come in. You can grab hold of this time of change and make it work for you as you "go through your life like a cellar and throw out everything that doesn't fit." Think of it as a striptease with you as the star performer.

I coached a woman once who told me that every morning she felt like she had a backpack of burdens that she just had to pick up and put on in order to start her day. Being weighted down with stuff was simply a part of getting up in the morning. I asked her to change her pattern, be a pattern-breaker, and instead of putting the backpack on, she could just put it over in the corner in her bedroom. She could still get to it if she felt she couldn't live without it. I asked her to give herself the chance to feel what it would be like to walk out of her room lightened up, free of the stuff, packing nothing on her back. This was a beginning for her, making conscious choices about how free she really wanted to be.

This too can be where your midlife adventure begins—playing with the idea of yourself as a shape-shifter and a pattern-breaker.

"Because her original pattern was so worn
The last time she flew apart,
She was forced to let the pieces
Reattach as they please.
Once the shock wore off,
She welcomed the change."

—Susan Mrosek

MAKE IT YOUR OWN

1. Unpack your backpack! What is outworn, outdated, and needless baggage?
2. Make a list of what no longer fits.
3. Design a ritual, a striptease, for getting rid of it.

"Re-examine all that you have been told...
dismiss that which insults your soul"

—Walt Whitman

Borderless Broads:

"What Was I Trained To Be and Who Am I Really?"

Being a borderless broad is a state of mind. It is also a *new* spiritual frontier for you.

Elizabeth Gilbert, in her book *Eat, Pray, Love*, speaks of the borderlands and people who live in these edge places as the "in-betweeners." Celtic mythology describes borderlands as "places where the veils are thin". They are power zones, fluid states of consciousness, where one walks between the worlds. It is not "gettable" with the rational mind. It is gettable with deep feminine instincts.

Many midlife women walk here comfortably because of their life experience and sheer number of years on the planet.

You become borderless when you are willing to ask "What was I **trained** to be and who am I really?"

This borderless state of mind allows outward identifying characteristics like philosophical "isms," nationalities, religious affiliations, body types, age, exclusive loyalty to family bloodlines, and other such externals to fall away. It is a place where all the baggage of identifications that have absorbed our energy through social training seems no longer to be relevant. Living through the social training of long ago is another way of dragging the backpack through our lives.

The borderless broad question: "**who am I really?"** answers you back from "the land of drop-aways," letting go of the customary identities and lives that have defined you up to this point.

The gifts of this state of being are many: fluidity and flexibility; freedom from labels, thoughts, and beliefs that imprison your natural curiosity; and eagerness to remain fresh and awake!

In its place, the adventure is to become women of the world, global nurturers to life within and without **wherever you find it**; to expand and radiate! This is a spiritual quest and a new frontier for this third destiny time!

MAKE IT YOUR OWN

1. What identifying characteristics did you take on through your early training and now assume to be part of you?
2. Which ones keep you from living fresh and awake? From walking between the worlds?
3. Write a description of what it would look like to be a "borderless broad." How would you feel? What would you do? Where would you live?

Do not censor yourself in any way.

Dream on, edge woman!

Are You Eating Your Wildness?

"In my house lives the most beautiful wild animal.
But she is sad.
She has lost her forest.
She has lost her tribe.
Her very language is almost gone, dissolved
In sorrow and disuse.
What can you do to comfort such a creature?
She stares out of the windows and longs to go somewhere—
But where?
The nothingness of thc days exhausts her.
Have you ever seen an animal weep?
When I touch her she looks at me with that
Lost world in her eyes—
Hopeful, but trembling."

—Mary Oliver

What is your wildness?

It's that part of you that births dreams, ideas, yearnings for adventure, the urge to create with true joy and exuberance.

The wildness in you belongs only to Nature. It comes from instinct, intuition, and dream states that have utterly no relation to the thinking mind. It is the unsettled, untamed, unrestrained you. It boasts familiarity with "edge" words like eccentric, notoriously odd, maverick, intense, ungovernable, emotional, restless, nomadic, and mystical. Magic is always afoot, and you are curiously curious!

Your wildness is your truest guide. It does not "color in the lines" or dress for success or obsess over kitchen cupboards. It laughs with abandon and weeps the same way.

Many of us are in the habit of eating our wildness! We have an inner ravenous beast that hungrily waits for our creative urges to bubble up, and then quickly devours them with the teeth of doubt, fear, and beliefs that limit what we think is possible.

I think we women have grown fat, cadaverous, and malnourished by eating the deepest hungers within us!

"The only people for me are the mad ones,
the ones who are mad to live, mad to talk, mad to be saved,
desirous of everything at the same time,
the ones who never yawn or say a commonplace thing,
but burn, burn, burn, like fabulous yellow roman candles
exploding like spiders across the stars..."

—Jack Kerouac

MAKE IT YOUR OWN

1. Your wildness has a voice. Invite it to speak to you, to tell you about itself.

2. Find a dream, an impulse to create, a yearning that has come to you more times than you can count and that you have "eaten" in fear or doubt.

3. Call together an "I refuse to eat my wildness" group. Declare to one another what you now claim as yours to express and what you are willing to do about it.

Reality Is Just a Collective Hunch

"We cannot live securely in a world that is not our own,
In a world interpreted for us by others.
An interpreted world is not a home.
Part of the terror is to take back our listening,
To put our ears to our own inner voices,
To see our own light.
It is our birthright,
And comes to us in silence."

—Elaine Bellezza,
article on Hildegard von Bingen

Our social training is a free gift, more or less, courtesy of our upbringing or down-bringing, as the case may be. It helps us navigate the everyday world of human interaction. It is, however, overrated as a source of identity. We often get stuck there, believing such training to be "the truth," prescribing to us the best way to behave, to live, to love, to be successful.

One night watching CNN will give you a good idea of what it is like to "live in a world interpreted for us by others." Lily Tomlin would counter that "reality is just a collective hunch." I would say it is all just a story: my version, your version, CNN's version...

When you reclaim your wildness, you take back your listening through your intuition and gut instincts. You listen to your body, which is always keenly ready to tell you the truth through the feeling states you experience. You make up your own stories that feel good and lighten you up. Your hunch is as good as anyone else's. You take back your listening in order to find your ground, your inner home. It is a supreme task of midlife to pay attention to this.

MAKE IT YOUR OWN

Your inner world is your own to create and nurture. It deeply affects the quality of your outer world.

1. Listen to some "crucial" bit of news on CNN or some other network. Play with the story. Rewrite your own version, your own ending—one that lightens you and makes you feel good. Practice trusting your OWN reality!
2. Take one circumstance in your life that is bothersome. Rewrite it with an ending that changes how you feel.
3. Do this in a group or with your family. Tell it to each other. Be outlandish. Go always for the best possible outcome! Expect the best in all the stories that touch your life. It is fun, and it literally changes your brain chemistry.
4. If you change the bothersome stories that come into your world, and create good feeling endings, you will, over time, change your inner and outer reality.

5 Becoming an Edge Woman

"A Woman needs a little madness or else she never dares cut the rope and be free."
—Zorba the Greek paraphrase

Live in between the worlds. Live in the borderlands. Shift from fully mainstream to edge living. The willingness "to take back [your own] listening" and pay attention to the condition of your own inner world requires a bit of madness. Let's define madness as that edge place where you are available to more than one reality. This is the making of a borderless broad. This is an edge woman, one who moves freely between realities, staying light and awake. She enjoys a bit of eccentricity as a way to "cut the rope and be free." An edge woman knows that no reality is the absolute truth. Mainstream is indeed only a collective hunch telling you what is real, what is to be feared, what is good, valuable, successful, or appropriate! An edge woman does not get caught here. She takes from the mainstream the practicalities that make life work and then she moves on to the edge places where greater wisdom and guidance reside: body, intuition, instincts, the wildness that is her birthright.

This is you, my borderless broad; a little madness keeps you zany, frisky, and humorous about who you really are and the experiences that come your way. Such madness fuels your courage, the courage to live differently and to feed your soul. It is colorful and exuberant. I do not think you can live full out without developing a bit of madness.

"My sister Emily loved the moors.
Flowers brighter than roses bloomed in the blanket of heath for her.
She found in bleak solitude many and dear delights
and the least and best loved was Liberty.
Liberty was the breath of Emily's nostrils;
without it she perished."

—Charlotte Bronte

MAKE IT YOUR OWN

Madness is a personal state of mind. It is an essential quality of freedom. Call it zaniness or eccentricity, if that works better for you, but cultivate it!

1. Think of yourself as an edge woman developing a bit of eccentricity, cultivating that feeling of freedom. How would your eccentricity express itself? In how you dress? Where you go? What you say? Is it some new creative outlet? Who are your friends?

2. What would it take for you to "cut the rope and be free?" (Don't over think this—just let it rip! Speak it to your mirror or lover or journal.)

Ladies in Waiting, the Age-Old Tale

"There is a daunting amount of life left—too much to squander.
She could not bear any longer simply to let time pass.
She wanted to live fully and properly."

—Joanna Trollope

Imagine a character you've seen countless times in stories, who stands in the middle of the room with hands thrust out front, forcefully yelling: *What* are you *waiting* for?" It's a very good question, and I am asking it of you now.

"Ladies in waiting" is a concept imprinted in the mind of most Western women. We grew up with tales of the English courts filled with such ladies always "waiting" at the beck and call of one royal pooh-bah or another. Remember, too, the story of Odysseus and his wife, Penelope. Penelope spends *20 years* waiting for Odysseus to return from his Odyssey as she whiles away her time spinning and waiting... and waiting some more.

It can be a real handicap, this habit of women waiting. Of course, if it is a choice made from knowing that the time is not right, then waiting is wisdom. If, however, waiting for life to show up day in and day out is a way of life...well, it's a bad dream leading to a future of more of the same.

Stories such as these that become part of our cultural assumptions are dangerous. They train us to hobble our spirits. Be wary of such stories. "Ladies in waiting" is only one of them.

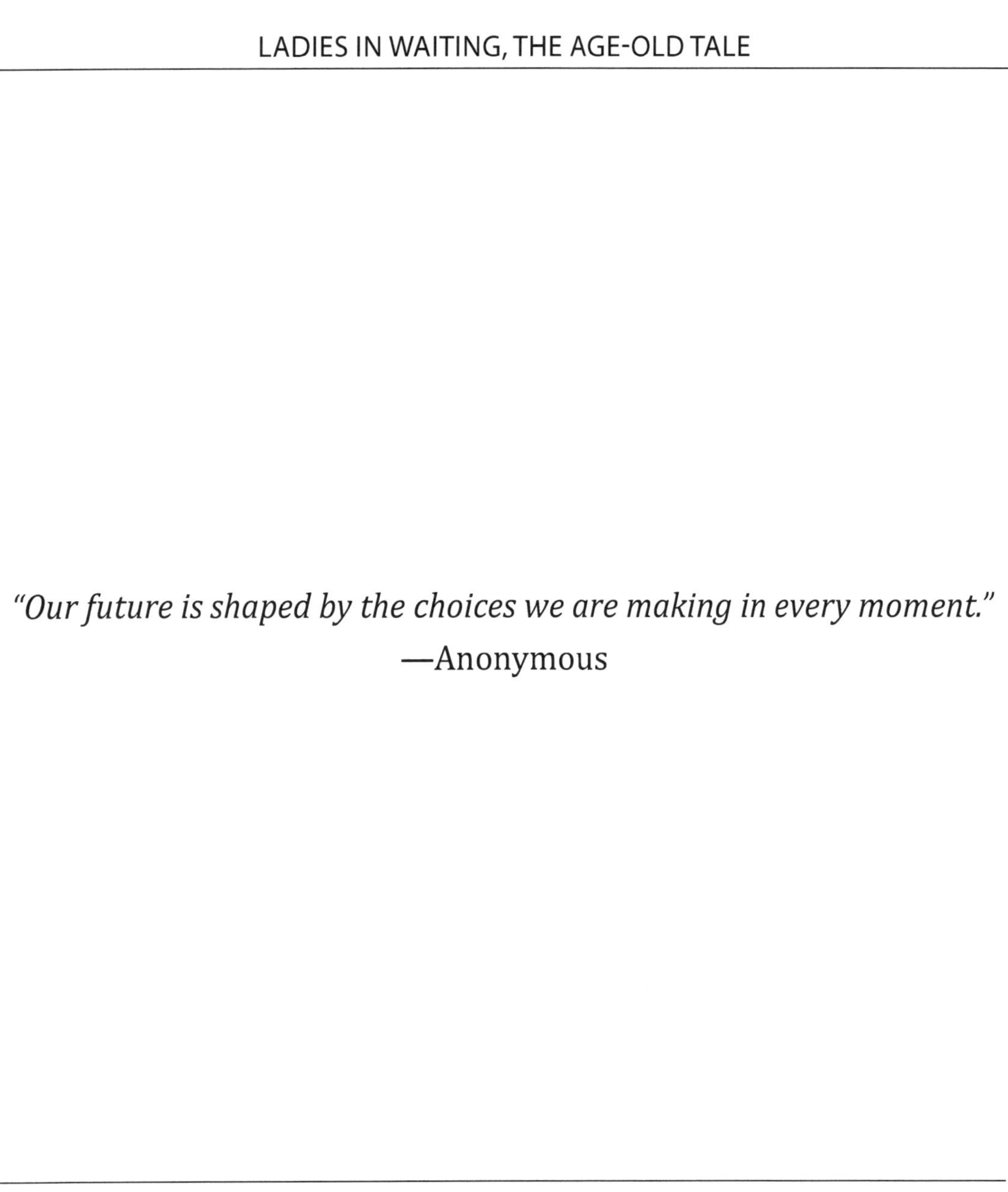

"Our future is shaped by the choices we are making in every moment."

—Anonymous

MAKE IT YOUR OWN

Being a lady in waiting is simply a wake-up call signaling that you need to change. Something wants to happen and only needs your forward motion to start the process.

1. Find a place in your life where "Penelope waiting and spinning" feels like your twin sister. Be bold. Ask yourself: What am I waiting for? Ask yourself: What are the chances of it showing up without some action on my part?
2. If you were willing to believe that you could stop waiting and take action, the first three things you would do are…
3. Repeat #2 for every "spin and wait" impulse you've got going in your life!
4. Repeat after me: "I no longer choose to *Penelope* my life." Now, put away the spinning wheel and just move, the rest will show up!

To Jump or Not, That Is the Question!

"There comes a time when everyone must make an act of power in order to proceed."

—Lynne Andrews

An intriguing thought, this. Are you awake to times when you knew that you could not proceed without making some act of power in order to take the next step or embrace the next change in your life?

I think we are often unconscious of these crossroad moments and their inherent power to change *absolutely everything.* Many times they just slip by because we are not alert to their power to course-correct our lives when we are confused, dulled out, tuned out, bored, or in some other foggy frame of mind.

If you are questioning your next steps, your path: whether to sell your house, leave a job or a relationship, or "take the habit," you are definitely at a crossroads moment.

The question to ask, then, is: What act of personal power is required of me in order to proceed? Usually the answer involves perceived risk and contains an element of fear, the impulse to do nothing, and an urge to just steady the boat, stay put, and make do—but you cannot!

Act of power moments are great gifts; they keep you wily, limber, and borderless.

The degree of suffering that you experience around these change times is most probably the result of thoughts and beliefs from tribal training we all received. Training that says: "I trained as a lawyer, doctor, Indian chief and that I will be until the end of my days. I pledged my life to this relationship and I will stick it out until death do us part. This is the kind of woman I am and I will be no other, no matter what."

One of the freest moments in my own life was when someone suggested to me that life was fluid and flexible *by nature* and that to stop the flow by agreeing to any fixed idea or vow, making life rigid and unchangeable, would most likely result in soul loss many times over before I actually left my physical body!

To jump or not to jump, that is the question. What say you?

MAKE IT YOUR OWN

1. It may be time for an act of power in your life, or maybe more than one, to get you to the next step. What might those acts be?
2. What course correction is most needed in your life at this time? Is it financial? Creative? Relational? Physical? Soulful?
3. If you are willing to feel the risk, face the fear, and keep moving through the impulse to avoid "rocking the boat," what are the first three things you would do?

My Mother Was Never Afraid of Color

I visited a client whose mother had just died. Entering the mother's home, I encountered walls filled with color: paintings of women, voluptuous women, with plump red lips and outrageously huge hats. Other paintings were of tropical scenes: trees laden with exotically plumed birds and feral animals peeking through the branches. "Nothing demure about this woman's world," I said. The daughter replied: *"My mother was never afraid of color."*

I told a friend this story, and the next time I saw her, she ran up to me, saying: "I thought about that 'not being afraid of color' thing, and I went home and painted all my walls with colors I love: bold colors, brilliant colors." Then she laughed.

I later saw a picture in a magazine of Samburu tribal women in Kenya. There they were, set against the deep blue of an African sky wearing wrap-around fabrics, all natural colors, all celebratory, all brilliant. The caption read: "Nature is not afraid of color." I spiraled right back in memory to the house long ago and the deceased midlife woman who had made her own life a palette of color.

Whether visiting a village in Kenya or the rooms of a suburban house in New Mexico, it was all the same, a "call to color." Creating a culture of color in your life engages the big energies of living. Choose dancers, musicians, and singers to pollinate your world. Choose stargazers, tarot readers, and nomadic, obsessed travelers to be your friends. Choose to be art and to do art, whatever that is for you.

No black-and-white world here. Enter the territory of edge women; women willing to walk in many worlds—worlds that create feeling states of freedom and laughter.

Your picture will obviously be different from mine. No matter. Just hang out where the color is.

"To be free, one must do free things!"
—Morgana Morgaine

MAKE IT YOUR OWN

Color can be a window into what your inner world looks like. It can also be a way to enhance the joy in your life.

1. Where do you stand on color? The best way to answer this is to look at your personal world: the clothes you wear, the walls and furnishings in your nest, the variety of friends and activities in your life, your lovemaking, the work that you do.

2. If you are afraid of color, you might ask yourself what decisions you have made about it. Are you afraid to stand out? Do you believe it is unprofessional to detour from basic black? Is there room for shades and blendings in your thoughts and beliefs, or does black-and-white thinking run your world?

3. If you choose to believe that "going color" would be liberating for you, an expression of inner freedom, what are the first three things you would do?

Flying Solo Gives You Windburn, Bugs in Your Teeth, *and* Chapped Lips!

When geese fly, each bird flaps its wings, creating an ***uplift*** for the bird immediately following. Flying in a V adds a greater flying range than if each bird ***flew on its own.*** When the lead goose fatigues, it rotates back into the formation and another goose steps up to lead position. Geese honk from behind, naturalists say, to ***encourage*** those up front to keep going. When a goose is injured or sick and falls out of formation, two geese drop out to follow and protect.

The life of a goose moves me to seek such an experience of support and wise use of group energy. I champion looking to nature for models of living and behaving that work. The goose, as does much of nature, teaches the folly of going it alone. It is a question of spirit, of life force, that makes this an inefficient way to live your life. We can only nurture and cheer ourselves on for so long as single birds! Solo is a lifestyle of diminishing returns. Creative expression suffers. Health suffers. The very nature of a human—to love and be love—suffers. We swim upstream when we go it alone.

Many of you in midlife are doing just that, some by choice and many as the result of the gander that died on you, divorced you (or vice versa), or other losses. If ever there was a circumstance that called on the best of edge women to break patterns and envision new lifestyles, this is it. Going beyond coupledom is the new normal in midlife, and our fear of the non-familial group is the only thing standing in our way to a richer and more productive life.

This topic is so important that I encourage you to read on as I explore with you the pattern-breaking factors of going from singling to commingling!

(Take note that 26 percent of all households are one-person households. Women make up over half such households, and most of the women are over 55. See www.suite101.com/content/when-single-again---should-you-live-alone-or-share-a-household-a279780 for the whole article.)

MAKE IT YOUR OWN

1. When are the times when you need or desire company? What would go easier for you in your life if you sacked "going solo"?
2. What are the fears you tell yourself about giving up going it alone? Are they real or the result of training?
3. Do you need lots of alone time? How can you expand your options to include both solo and together in your lifestyle choices?

Kinship Can Be Learned, and Blood Family Is NOT the New Normal

"Happiness is a gift and the trick is not to expect it,
but delight in it when it comes and to add to other people's store of it.

What happens if too early we lose a parent, that party on whom we rely for only... everything! What did these people do when their families shrank? They cried their tears, but then they did the ***vital*** *thing. They built a new family, person by person. They came to see that family need not be defined merely as those with whom they have blood, but as those for whom they would give their blood!"*

—Charles Dickens, *Nicholas Nickleby*

In Africa, kinship groups are being created for orphaned animals. Animal documentaries show young zebras and elephants being rescued and raised by humans until of an age to be slowly introduced into engineered species-specific kinship groups. Animals birthed in different herds, sharing no bloodlines, are able to bond with each other and thrive in newly created ***family*** groups, providing the same support, nurturance, and protection as an original family grouping.

It takes time and patience, naturalists say, but safety nets of new families can be created among non-related individuals.

Now, this is really good news. You may feel fiercely protective of your freedom, your individual self, and your privacy, but this does not negate the fact that we all need support, nurturing, and even protection at times. It is possible to have one's privacy and sense of self and still develop new kith and kin! Why in the world would increasing numbers of women in midlife "go it alone" when the richness of a shared life, shared work, shared laughter is an option for adventurers embracing "the wisdom of the goose."

If you are a believer in "soul recognition," you have had the experience of knowing that you have met certain people and felt a special affinity for them: a recognition of ease and comfort in their presence. Maybe you shared previous lifetimes—or not. Whatever the case may be, finding such souls is a gift and the rich beginning of a new kinship family.

What a remarkable path to becoming a borderless broad and pattern-breaker extraordinaire. This is edge work for edge women inspired to create the new normal.

If the zebra and the elephant can do it, why not you?

MAKE IT YOUR OWN

1. Are there people in your life right now with whom you might create a new family?
2. Even if you do not choose to live in some collective way, are there ways to create extended family through shared projects, play, or spiritual pursuits?
3. If you believe in "soul recognition," what might it feel like when it happens? If you become conscious of this possibility, it may just begin to show up!

11 Pod Living Makes for Prosperous Women

From herds to pods, the elephants have it!

"The wild psyche can endure exile. It makes a woman go on looking, and if she cannot find the culture that encourages her, then she usually decides to construct it herself. That is good, for if she builds it, others who have been looking for a long time will mysteriously arrive one day enthusiastically proclaiming that they have been looking for this all along."

—Clarissa Pinkola Estes, *Women Who Run With Wolves*

What is most compelling about liberating your lifestyle is the tremendous opportunity you have to create smaller cultures within the larger culture that meet your needs for a joyful, meaningful, nourishing, soulful habitat! The larger culture in which you live is incapable of providing the unique circumstances that help you thrive. It is by nature a lumbering bureaucratic mainstream structure designed to keep the greatest number of people afloat—or not.

When life becomes most precious and every day a gift just because you are breathing and the birds are flying and the rain is falling and it is a great big "YES, let me at this day" feeling when you wake up in the morning, this is the time to settle for nothing less than the people and the environment that brings out the best of what you are and have to give. It is the time to ensure that your soul has the optimum conditions to express itself in the world, which necessarily means hooking up to the greater cosmic wonder in a profound way as a *midlife mystic*. Your gifts, your talents, and your soul's vitality require certain conditions to flourish. It is like a garden where a particular plant needs certain soil conditions, amounts of water, levels of warmth through sun or shade, and frequencies of light. To live consciously and well is to *know* what you need to thrive and to construct the culture that supports it. This requires others. This requires a pod!

I write about animals because they seem to have retained behaviors and lifestyles that we have lost or never had. Particularly inspiring is the female elephant. I love their size, their deliberateness, their dedication to the extended family with a cooperative care ethic that protects the young and the vulnerable. I love their deep body rumblings that travel for miles, keeping a connection with one another. I love their seeming remembrance of the dead, the ritual of fondling the bones of herd members long gone.

Elephants seem to live life ***taking care***. Led by an older matriarch who guides daughters, sisters, and other mothers, these quiet beings walk the Earth together from birth until death, ***taking care***. When danger threatens, the older fit females raise their great heads and trunks skyward, facing outward toward the intruder, and form a circle with the young, old, and vulnerable in the center. They trumpet loudly, rushing forward just enough to clearly communicate: "back off"!

As a further point of interest, the young males stay until they reach a certain age and then join the other guys, coming around the females only "when sex is in the air." A great arrangement for midlife women, from my perspective!

In Kenya, a group of Samburu tribal women were banished from their village after being forcibly raped. This apparently was a circumstance that shamed the tribe. (Go figure!) These women set up a village of their own called Umoja (Unity) and transformed from abused women into healthy and empowered mothers, daughters, and sisters. They set up a tourism economy selling their traditional crafts and performing ritual dances for travelers to Africa. Word spread of their success and other women from other tribes came to join, leaving similar abusive situations. They now thrive, sharing life and pooling their resources. What about the men? A Samburu resident says: "We are not monks, our boyfriends visit and then leave…" (Hmmmm, the elephants do indeed have it!)

Midlife *is* a time to expand one's options, to seek out the best possible lifestyle design that allows you to thrive and to create the freedom for living your life full out. Might you see yourself living in a pod of women, sharing a large home, creating pockets of privacy mixed with playful spaces to share life? What about a cluster of small cottages with common areas?

Imagine remodeling empty churches, schools, warehouses, or million-dollar homes gone bust and undertaking the adventure of creating pods. Imagine yourself pooling resources for the basic needs, enjoying deep emotional bonds, and "tending life" in single and shared forms through whatever passionate pursuits you enjoy. Imagine thinking bigger and creating habitats in service of the greater life beyond your life. Imagine you "pod up" with sister-creatives, be they gardeners, entrepreneurs, travelers, writers, textile enthusiasts, color artists, theatrical people, spiritual seekers, contemplatives, or scholars—whoever is called to your tribe!

So much power, motivation, energy, and focus, so many ideas come from shared vision. Momentum is exponentially increased, and the opportunity for greater joy is without bounds.

Imagine pods of prosperous women in service to self and each other, living life full out.

Read on, midlife mavens. The Beguines await!

"I'm singing in my labor and I can hear you and all women singing with me."

—Anonymous

MAKE IT YOUR OWN

1. Spend some time imagining what kind of a pod would work for you. Pods are a fun image, whimsically speaking. Might it be an option for you?
2. If you were creating a culture that would encourage and support you, what might it look like? What needs would you want it to meet?
3. What would you want to give from your wealth of gifts and talents?

Begin the Beguine: Middle Ages Wisdom for Middle Life YOU!

"A remarkable movement emerged in Europe that became known as the Beguinage (begeenahj) Communities. Thousands of women who did not want to marry or take the veil began to set themselves up in female collectives."

—Karen Maitland, *The Owl Killers*

Thirteenth century Europe birthed an outstanding group of women calling themselves Beguines (*begeens*). They organized themselves in response to the limited options of the time, which were marriage, the convent, or the "street." They were Catholic-identified, as religion was the primary definer of one's life during this age in Europe. Whether Jewish women joined, I do not know.

What set the Beguines apart was their independence, their mystical and artistic leanings, and their savvy at setting up economies that worked for vast numbers of women. They were educators of girls, hospice tenders, poets, writers, textile makers, guild organizers, and more. Some established their guilds in textile-rich northern Europe by virtue of the influence of their sheer numbers and organizational power. Some Beguines were supported by wealthy patronesses who bought houses or otherwise supported the Beguine lifestyle. Some cities boasted 3,000 plus members living in enclaves.

Four or five women or more might live in one house; others lived in larger convent-like communities. Their particular sense of kinship was shaped by their religious commitment; most of these women did not share a blood lineage and bonded through shared values. They treasured most keenly their mystical belief that direct relationship with their sense of the divine was possible, rather than having to go through the intermediary of "priest and power" mandated by the Church.

Most importantly, in their visionary wisdom, the Beguines willed their houses to one another so that "Beguine would always take care of Beguine"; a safety net created far in advance of our thinking today.

What a splendid model. Here is inspiration for a major shift to liberate your lifestyle, become a borderless broad, push the envelope, court the edge, and be you!

MAKE IT YOUR OWN

Here's where the pedal hits the metal!

1. Imagine yourself "liberating your lifestyle" from whatever constraints you see shaping your life now. Financial issues? Loneliness? Lack of a "stage" for your creativity and experience? Passion for some kind of meaningful work with others?

2. Just spend some time sitting with "new options for a new normal," a revolution in lifestyles for midlife women.

3. Engage other women in conversations about this. Call together a meet-up group and see who shows up. It is an adventure. Explore and expand your options!

Midlife Mavericks and Money Miracles

"A good dinner is of great importance to good talk.
One cannot think well, love well, or sleep well, if one has not dined well.
The lamp in the spine does not light on beef and prunes."

—Virginia Woolf

If you find this quote confusing, it may be due to the sensibilities of a different century. Virginia was born in 1882. To my mind, what Virginia Woolf was saying is that to live an illuminated life, one must have enough money to eat well and thus live well. A diet of "beef and prunes" (a contemporary equivalent might be a diet of macaroni and cheese) does not light the lamp of wisdom (kundalini) in the spine and lend itself to healthy thinking or living!

I use this as a jumping-off point for the radical idea that poverty is NOT an option. Poverty continues because we are willing to tolerate it individually and collectively.

We operate from a well-oiled axiom that "the poor will always be with us": a belief that keeps us stuck in a brain rut of limited thinking and limited options.

Here is an example of limited option thinking from a recent online newsletter. In the article "Life After 50: Women's Worst Fear After 50? It's Not What You Think" Barbara Hannah Grufferman writes:

> The one common thread that linked their [women's] thoughtful comments [in a poll she conducted] was this: *the fear of not having enough money as they get older.....*
>
> The disturbing thing is that financial destitution could end up being more than just a fear for far too many women in this country; it could become a fact.
>
> **What's the solution?** Help women over 50 get and keep jobs, and give them access to affordable health care so that they can continue to have productive lives for as long as they wish...**Women over 50 must be given the opportunity to continue working or return to the workforce so that the fear of poverty (for themselves and their families) does not become a reality.**

Our culture, more or less, sees financial security as an individual pursuit relying solely on one's own labor as part of the workforce. This *is* part of the solution, given the world we live in, but we merrily skip over ancillary options like joining forces, embracing the power of pooling, the *one for all and all for one* thinking that makes successful security more likely.

It is ironic to me that in an affluent culture like our own, we tend to go down the well-trod one-way road that relies on the individual to make her own fortune. Collective ideas are met with suspicion and evoke knee-jerk assumptions like

"Here we go again, that wretched socialism raising its ugly head!" Never mind that the individual solution to economics does not seem to work for the majority. In contrast, other countries like India have a more collective response to moving from surviving to thriving. The Grameen bank, for example, is offering a way out of poverty for countless women and their families by enlisting **collectives of women** to support one another as they use individual and collective small loans to create businesses that lift everyone up! It is a village concept because the Grameen model relies on the power of the collective and uses the power of relationships to succeed.

Some years ago, I sat in a café in Santa Fe, New Mexico, wracking my brain with "the money question." This was long before organizations like "MoveOn" creatively commandeered the Web to raise money.

I envisioned clusters of people coming together to create financial solvency by pooling money and resources. Using the formula "small amounts of money coming from **large** numbers of people" instead of the old story of a **few** wealthy giving to the many, I imagined 5,000 women investing $5.00 per week for 52 weeks and accruing $1.3 million. A total flip of the mainstream model for raising and controlling wealth. Imagine such clusters peppering the planet!

Then there is the emotional question of moving from "mine" to "mutual"; not so easy for us, and yet, it opens doors to new possibilities. It goes even further in removing mental and physical fences that keep us stuck in limited options. Unequivocally borderless broad thinking!

Granted, we all choose to have some degree of ownership—the "mine" in our lives—but the extreme we see today keeps us stuck in owning and maintaining one of everything, much of which could easily be shared and money saved for individual passionate pursuits like travel. Well, that is my agenda anyway!

Isn't it interesting that our language contains terms like "mutual funds" and "commonwealth" and yet it seems that we only feel safe using this terminology anonymously on Wall Street.

Imagine, borderless broad (that's you), becoming a midlife maverick creating new frontiers in finance and collective well-being!

"Alice laughed. 'There's no use trying,' she said.
'One can't believe impossible things.'

'I daresay you haven't had much practice,' said the Queen.
'When I was your age, I always did it for half an hour a day.
Why, sometimes I've believed as many as six impossible things before breakfast.'"

—Lewis Carroll, *Alice in Wonderland*

MAKE IT YOUR OWN

1. I suggest Victoria Castle's book, *The Trance of Scarcity,* to examine your own relationship to poverty and affluence. Gather a group and use her workbook.

2. If "pooling" were an option for you in some parts of your life, what would it look like? Where would you begin?

3. How might you follow the Beguine model? Would you be a patroness in some way? Can you see yourself willing money or houses to continue Beguine-like enclaves?

4. Is there some area of your life where you might participate in the "small amounts of money/large numbers of people" thinking?

5. Begin the conversation. Money is a creative force, and there are countless forms it can take when we break out of the conventional economic thinking we were conditioned to believe.

Men Wander, Women Nest—What to Do?

Woman #1: *"It certainly keeps one from the entire male-female dance of misunderstanding and destruction, doesn't it? But I do think it all comes down to bonding in the end: this problem we seem to have with men. Women bond, men don't. It's to do with biology and we'd probably all be better off if we could simply cope with living in herds or prides or whatever; one male of the species sniffing up a dozen females with the females accepting this as the course of life."*

Woman #2: *"They reproduce while he what? Fetches home the dead whatever for breakfast?"*

Woman #1: *"They are a sisterhood. He's window dressing. He services them but they bond to each other. It's a thought."*

Woman #2: *"Isn't it just!"*

—Elizabeth George, Mystery Writer

How many women have you met whose husbands left them at a certain age or had affairs during their marriage? Women weep and wail and talk of trust issues with friends and therapists. They go to marriage counseling with the offending husband in hopes of getting the magic back.

Many of these women say the same things: "I don't understand why it happened. I was a good wife. I put him through school. We had a good sex life." And on and on and on.

This is one of those issues that makes me wonder... I wonder why the same social melodrama repeats itself over and over, for centuries actually, without anyone saying "Wait a minute, what's *really* going on here?"

Here's my take on it, although let it be said that I am writing in *general* terms—exceptions abound. Nevertheless, it is definitely the elephant in the living room, madly trying to get someone's attention and never quite talked about head-on!

I believe it is man's nature to seek sex with more than one female even after declaring undying fidelity in marriage. Man's biology is at play. I believe it is woman's nature to live in supportive relational groupings where women and children are cared for by more than the "nuclear family" and/or the efforts of a single mother. Of course, women often seek sex with more than one partner also. It is biology, not morality.

Instead of women beating their chests and reliving the story about the "husband gone astray," doesn't it make more sense for women to enjoy the support and camaraderie of care with other women and have a relationship with a man or men (if that is your preference) that does not assume undying fidelity and continuous presence (which is pretty much a fantasy anyway)?

Let it be said that since we live in human cultures with money as the primary safety net, fathers of children must be strenuously legally bound to provide *more* than adequate funds to care for the mother and children. It is part of the responsibility equation for "making babies"!

In short, options are what it is all about. This may or may not be your way of doing life, but it definitely would loosen the stranglehold on many women who "cannot leave him" because of fear, fears like "How would I support my kids? Where would I go? How will I support myself as I age?"

Women might use their nest-building expertise and safety net savvy to avoid economic traps. Animals instinctively create safety nets called herds, families, flocks, and pods. They never give a thought to being a "victim." I think we ought to take a look at what works in Nature and follow suit...break patterns, and create option-filled lifestyles that benefit men and women alike.

So, perhaps you can see yourself leaping the borders, flirting with the edge, and liberating your lifestyle, this way or another way!

MAKE IT YOUR OWN

1. Write or talk about why you felt all defensive about this chapter. What limits did you come up against within yourself? What romance story reared its head, saying: "Yes, but…"
2. Perhaps it was a relief to hear this—freeing somehow. Go with that. Talk about that to a trusted friend or group.
3. What lifestyle might really feed your soul and create a greater sense of support and ease?
4. If finances are an issue, what new options can you come up with? Can you change your world view from how you think it should be to what works best for you?

Hang Your Life on What Counts

"I live in the most ideal situation for a writer.
I dwell in the midst of creative souls who encourage
others to pursue their own visions, dreams, and passions.
I have discovered that such a strong feminine atmosphere
affirms and nurtures..."

—Laura Swan, *The Forgotten Desert Mothers*

I happened on a little book years ago written by an inspiring educator, Dolores Leckey. She nailed it for me by articulating structures that help women thrive without the rigidity of mindless rules and regulations! Her little book, *Women and Creativity*, was one of those that fell off the shelf and into my visionary dreams of what could be.

Dolores says that women's creativity is enhanced and sustained by structures that:

- Allow for spiritual exploration by providing time and space and study opportunities.
- Evoke community, where life ***can be shared*** and consciousness enhanced.
- Articulate common purpose.
- Provide opportunities for solitude where the soil of creativity can be cultivated, where seeds barely formed can take root and be protected and nourished until strong enough to become visible.

Much later, I found another woman's thoughts on life enhancement. I am notorious for not knowing where I pick up such gems. They just end up on sticky notes in file folders, a bad habit when one goes to write a book and give credit where credit is due!

This wise being said that to maintain one's center, one needs:

- Room to feel and stillness to simply quiet the mind and body enough to even begin to feel.
- Cleanliness, order, sunlight, warmth, and spacious vistas in one's immediate environment.
- Regularity in sleep and wake patterns in harmony with the seasons.
- Balanced scheduled meals in easy company.
- Daily direct connection with nature, grounding and re-energizing the soul.

What we hang our life on is like the wire armature a sculptor uses to give form and shape to the clay.

What we hang our life on determines the quality of our life. If we tend to those elements that generate and support a life of creativity, health, and deep spiritual peace, we are freed to use our life force to express full out, to "spend" ourselves as a precious currency in our work, in our loving, in our everyday joy.

MAKE IT YOUR OWN

Conscious lifestyles require breaking the pattern of old worn-out habits, structures, and dreams and replacing them with what really supports us.

1. What would you like to hang your life on?
2. If what is written in this chapter resonates with you, then write about how that would look in your particular life.
3. What common purpose might be the glue that held your life with that of others together?

Nix the Female Culture of Flaws

"I began to discover my inner voice, to listen to my own values, desires, and passions. I was invited to listen to my feelings, emotions, and inner stirrings for the wisdom they contain. I discovered the freedom to stop hauling around the dead wood that had burdened me, the ***shoulds*** *and the* ***oughts****, the quiet tyrant within that tells me I am not good enough."*

—Laura Swan, *The Forgotten Desert Mothers*

A coaching client said to me: "Yes, but how do I learn to love myself when I've spent a lifetime noticing what's ***wrong*** with me?"

I know very few Western women of any age who would not resonate with this question.

It seems to have been a dedicated practice of the Puritans and other like-minded sects to create a religious milieu that accentuated the flaws in human beings—

women, in particular—resulting in a language rife with thoughts of "not enough-ness," *a language of starvation*. The litany of beliefs many of us carry shows up in a language peppered with: "I am not good enough, attractive enough, smart enough, successful enough, white enough, black enough, Swedish enough." And so it goes...

The deeper underbelly to this kind of thinking comes to Western women from our European female ancestors where the words "I am the least of these" can be found in the "languaging" of many genius women. For example, Sor Juana of Mexico, a scientist, theologian, and all-around woman of brilliance, spoke of herself as "I am the least of these." Hildegard von Bingen, German Abbess, composer, visionary, and all-around woman of brilliance ingratiated herself as a "mere woman" in conversations with power brokers of the Church. Even Queen Elizabeth the First, authoress of a Golden Age for England used the "I, a mere woman" to charm and placate her male counterparts. It is a legacy that has insinuated itself into the female psyche for generations and continues to show up in our daughters as well, a fact brought home to me in my coaching practice.

This language of diminishment is a "leech" upon the creative psyche of women. It is starvation-making, siphoning off the vitality of our days and the brilliance that we bring to this world. It shows up in neon lights around the obsession with weight issues sucking energy, like a high-voltage grid, from many of us. It shows up in the reticence "to be seen" and to step out with authority in the world. Even women who are "out there" in the world in power positions still smart from that tiny voice that hungrily attacks with messages like: "Don't get too big for your boots" or "What do *you* know, really?"

You are most likely largely unconscious of these "habits of harm," so ingrained are they.

Nixing the female culture of flaws means deflating your mistaken belief that perfection is something to aspire to, or that it is even possible. Perfection thinking is toxic. It sends your creative energy down a yellow brick road looking for a wizard to make you whole and good enough. It creates the illusion that a state of perfection is ordered and predictable and achievable—that our lives will be perfect once we are perfect!

One antidote lies in creating some symbolic practice that reminds you that human perfection is illusion. Consider women weavers in some indigenous cultures who always weave an imperfection into their rugs. They deliberately "mess up" the pattern or weave a different color into the mix; a small flaw intentionally created. Why? As a reminder that only the gods are perfect, that there is perfection in imperfection, that so-called flaws are a part of the larger scheme of cosmic perfection .

So, ENOUGH! Nix the female culture of flaws! Stop it! It is an ancestral hanger-on, an insidious training tactic that does not serve borderless broads. Conversations about weight, face-lifts, and how to be the perfect anything diminish who you are. They take the "magnum opus," the great work, that is YOU as a spiritual being in human form and make your life small and confined.

"It is only with the heart that one can see rightly;
What is essential is invisible to the eye."

—Antoine de St. Exupery

The Cracked Pot, A Story

A water bearer in India had two large pots hung on each end of a pole that he carried across his neck. One of the pots had a crack in it, and while the other pot was perfect and always delivered a full portion of water at the end of the long walk from the stream to the master's house, the cracked pot arrived only half full. For two years, this went on daily, with the bearer delivering only one and a half pots full of water to his master's house. Of course, the perfect pot was proud of its accomplishments, perfect for the end for which it was made. But the poor cracked pot was ashamed of its own imperfection and miserable that it was able to accomplish only half of what it had been made to do.

After two years of what it perceived to be a bitter failure, it spoke to the water bearer one day by the stream. "I am ashamed of myself, and I want to apologize to you."

"Why?" asked the bearer. "What are you ashamed of?"

"I have been able, for these past two years, to deliver only half my load because this crack in my side causes water to leak out all the way back to your master's house. Because of my flaws, you have to do all of this work, and you don't get full value from your efforts," the pot said.

The water bearer felt sorry for the old cracked pot, and in his compassion he said, "As we return to the master's house, I want you to notice the beautiful flowers along the path."

Indeed, as they went up the hill, the old cracked pot took notice of the sun warming the beautiful wild flowers on the side of the path, and this cheered it some. But at the end of the trail, it still felt bad because it had leaked out half its load, and so again it apologized to the bearer for its failure.

The bearer said to the pot, "Did you notice that there were flowers only on your side of your path, but not on the other pot's side? That's because I have always known about your flaw, and I took advantage of it. I planted flower seeds on your side of the path, and every day while we walk back from the stream, you've watered them. For two years I have been able to pick these beautiful flowers to decorate my master's table. Without you being just the way you are, he would not have this beauty to grace his house."

—Author Unknown, India

Now, aren't you glad you are a "cracked pot" too?

MAKE IT YOUR OWN

1. What language of starvation do you use against yourself? Be specific.
2. Become conscious, and stop it. Use some tactile trigger like raising your hand in a gesture of STOP or utter an "Oh, no, I am not going there" each time until you disconnect from these habits of harm!
3. In seeking to be perfect, what experiences have you missed out on?
4. How would you feel, what would you do, how would you act, if you believed you were "good enough"?

17

Harems & Healing

Get a group!

"In the harem, women can relax their guard, because they know that no men will enter the area. As a result, the harem was often a lively and fun place in the era when women isolated themselves at home. Women could dress more casually, sing and tell stories, and meet with other women from the area. Friends and neighbors traditionally socialized with each other in the harem, bringing young children and eating snacks and tea. In homes with servants, the servants would attend the women in the harem, and in large households, servants might play music and offer other entertainments."

—www.WiseGeek.com/what-is-a-harem.htm

I am fascinated by the idea of harems as another way women once bonded and shared in a collective social structure. Far from the popular misconception of a harem as a group of women waiting at the beck and call of a male who seeks to be "serviced," a harem offered a space for female bonding and letting your hair down.

It is fair to say that women are very often the carriers and perpetuators of the female culture of flaws. As the primary messengers of cultural values in the home—birthing babies and raising daughters, in particular—you may, unconsciously or not, pass on the legacy of criticalness and not enough-ness. You may also be aware how we injure each other by our off-the-cuff assessments of each other, our bodies, our looks, the externals—a form of comparison shopping, to be sure!

I once visited an island resort very popular with German nationals. Every day a new plane load would arrive, among them many midlife women. I would see these women— tanned and topless, often Reubenesque in shape, gold chains about their necks, large bare breasts bouncing, bikini bottoms holding ample derrieres—walking the beach. They walked easily and proudly, their ampleness for all to see and appreciate. I loved it! I was inspired by it! How refreshing to see women happy in their bodies, laughing and talking and soaking up the sun.

I visited a woman's bathhouse in Morocco where women went every Friday night to scrub up before the weekend holy day. Women of every shape, size, and age, all wildly soaping each other amid buckets of flying rinse water, enjoying the din of conversation and laughter. How liberating, natural, easy, and open!

For those of us schooled in knee-jerk evaluations of the female body and the aging female body, in particular, I say: embrace "Harems of Healing," private spaces to free the flaws, to nurture and celebrate our aging, perfectly imperfect bodies!

It is all about lightening up, midlife mavens. Opting for wholeness, self–acceptance, and just plain fun…skinny, corpulent, heavy-breasted, or "floppy puppy ears," as my grandfather used to call my grandmother's breasts. My mother even vacuumed in pantyhose and high heels, bless her. It's all the stuff of merriment and seriously unserious mayhem!

MAKE IT YOUR OWN

1. Consider creating a space with other women where you can meet to groom one another and play. Shampoo and brush hair, do toenails, lotion backs, be openly nude, and learn to relax. Share a mutually-created bathhouse experience.

2. Consider upping the ante as you become familiar with one another and intentionally tell each other what you like about each other's bodies. Tell each other what you like about your own body! Move on to what you like about the inner you, your essential soulful selves.

3. BREATHE. BE PRESENT. Squirming is allowed, because we tend to want to disassociate from such an unfamiliar focus. It will change with familiarity. You are learning to become undefended and live life full out!

4. Play around with dressing differently. Push your limits to include more color and spacious flowing clothing. How we dress is another indicator of how we view ourselves and how much we are willing to reveal. Help each other to stretch in expanding how you see yourselves. Does your clothing restrict movement? Do you hide in unremarkable colors or fabrics? Are you always dressed for business?

Sex & Spirit: The Alchemy of Woman's Power

Imagine in midlife, without the baby thing, or the extreme "how I look" thing, or the perfect lover thing, you turn your sex life into an expanded experience of *Life as lover*. You use the playful surrender of sex to tumble headlong into the vaster universe of belonging to something so much greater. You become a midlife mystic taking your human lover along for the ride. He or she will most likely welcome the adventure!

In its most human expression, sex can be an experience of bubble, bubble, toil and trouble, reminiscent of Macbeth's witches, or it can be a *way in,* a way in to the vast universe whose very nature is to connect, to join, to merge—a nature we humans very much share.

Next time you make love really well, experiencing it as deeply satisfying and encountering moments of real oneness, *know* that you have tapped into something infinite. You have tapped into your power to go beyond separateness. If you can go beyond separateness, for even just a few sexual moments, then you can expand that skill into experiencing immersion with all creation, becoming her lover, never her destroyer.

Sex gives you the opportunity to practice connection with the whole of yourself, your body, your emotions, and in some mysterious way, your subtle energy field. Sexual expression gives you a glimpse into a "higher octave" relationship. Through it, you see the possibility of joining with the whole of the physical world and the creatures you encounter, human and otherwise, as well as the worlds of the unseen. You see that ecstasy is possible; it is the utter joy you feel *naturally* in states of merging, connecting, and joining.

This is the stuff of mystics, this desire for a deep, direct, and total-person experience of connection. This connection is also the stuff of woman's nature.

Such alchemy of sex and spirit transforms. It compels us to express the deepest of loves, a love that vows a positive and caring relationship to all life. It can make the experience of separation unbearable.

MAKE IT YOUR OWN

1. Observe the quality of your sexual expression and the feeling of connection or absence thereof. No judgments. Just visit here and "take stock."

2. If you have said to yourself: "I know there is more to sex," what might it be that you are yearning for?

3. You might identify with being a midlife mystic. If you do, journal about your sense of the power of sexual connection and the yearning for spiritual union. How might the one experience open into the other for you?

Trust Is a Train

"Long ago, railroad tracks were laid through the Alps from Vienna to Venice, way before there was ever a train, because they KNEW that one day a train would come."

—*Under the Tuscan Sun*, movie

It is the custom to talk about emotional states like trust as some commodity that one can get and then have. Once we've got it, then we can proceed to do certain things (whatever they are) that we could not do otherwise. It's another one of those "ladies in waiting" games like "When I lose weight, I will..." or "When I have trust, I will...be open or spend the money to...or..." (fill in the blank).

The truth is that living life full out is about creating a "living trust," meaning it is an active process. In order to feel trust, one has to practice it without knowing when the train will show up!

You may be caught in a mind-set that makes big changes terrifying because life seems more finite at this end of the age spectrum. Risking money for something that is not "bread and butter" or letting go of lots of stuff accumulated over the years can conjure up real terror. Is this logical? Well, I think it is.

Life is different in midlife. Perhaps you are winding down on generating income to some extent. It is a natural inclination to pull back and preserve what you have. You might be asking: "What will I have left if I give away what I have accumulated? What will I do if I spend this money on something I yearn for and there is no money coming in to replace it? What if something happens?"

I know this place. I have been up against it several times when ideas of my safety and security ran smack into deep yearnings, calls that I felt I wanted to answer.

I now wonder if midlife does not require more trust than any other time, as life seems more immediate, more time-sensitive.

What I have discovered is that holding on to anything with a "just in case" attitude rapidly depletes energy and joy. Life becomes smaller, less adventuresome.

Playing it safe as a lifestyle just may be the source of inertia and unhappiness I see in many women's faces. There are many times when to remain alive—that is, exuberant and engaged—you have to practice trust so deeply that you go ahead and "lay the track" before knowing whether a train will show up or not.

You have to live the unknown, juggling trust side-by-side with the fear factor. There is just no other way to go from ***safe and numb*** to ***leap and live.***

Oh, by the way, did you hear the story about the town that was suffering from a seemingly never-ending drought? One evening, all the farm families decided to meet up at the church to pray for rain. A long line of people snaked their way toward the church door. In that line walked one lone little girl carrying an umbrella!

EXPECT THE BEST!

MAKE IT YOUR OWN

1. Where do you need to show up in your life, umbrella in hand, trusting that doing what you deeply yearn to do will bring the much-needed rain into your life?
2. If you feel dry, predictable, and stuck, there is a track out there somewhere that needs laying. What's in the way of your trust to begin?
3. If you knew you could not fail, what would you do next? The first three actions would be…

Courageous Conversations

"Fear is the cheapest room in the house.
I would like to see you living in better conditions."

—Hafiz

"One thing I've learned is that the only way I can create the kinds of conversations I want to have with people is to GO FIRST and share something personal and meaningful about my own life...then actually inquire into the life of the one I'm with, ask a question that really takes us somewhere."

—Jan Phillips

Choosing to see your world as a friendly place saves a lot of wear and tear. You suffer emotional extremes and limited thinking by seeing the world as threatening, mean, and fearsome. The payoff is only misery. Edge women choose to see their world as friendly, option-filled, and bursting with opportunities to connect in nourishing relationships. They live this.

I think it is time to rewrite the rules of engagement, changing our assumptions regarding how we go about forming bonds with each other. Asking more from "the art of relationship" only enriches our experience. It is obvious that many of our contacts are simply interactions motivated by transactions and negotiations to smooth the course of daily life. Much of what passes for relationship is simply a thin veneer of connection, shallow at best, that leaves us feeling depleted, bored, and hardly engaged. What a waste.

Training may have taught you that "real" relationships take a long time to develop and involve some level of jockeying around as you feel the other out, testing levels of safety and trust.

What if you realize that this *is* just learned etiquette that can be changed? What if you break the pattern and "cut to the chase"? What if you rely on *gut instinct and intuition* to tell you if a potential bond is worth pursuing? What if you pay attention to what your body and more subtle senses reveal?

"Cut the crap" has new meaning in midlife. Life *is* shorter and oh, the bliss of feeling like you just said what you meant and just busted through the expected propriety. You know the interaction was great because you actually ended a conversation feeling energized, free, and real. You were borderless; you were on the edge!

Try these radical rules of engagement to introduce a sense of liveliness and create experiences that actually hold your attention, lighten you up, and leave you wanting more!

- Get to know someone a whole lot faster by looking them in the eye (squirming is OK, as we usually have to override some primitive brain structure that avoids this) and read what's there with your gut.

- Tell friends/lovers/family that you are on a new adventure into courageous conversation and issue an invitation to participate. (Make it clear that either party can choose to say no.)
- Practice radical transparency. It looks something like this: "I want to tell you what I know about myself at this moment. It will help you to know me. I will update you as needed because I change. I would like the same from you."
- Say what you mean even when it makes your stomach "go south." Courageous conversation is staying current with you and the other person in the conversation.
- Let go, let go, let go. Your energy depends upon it! Be breathless with the edginess you are now allowing into your life. What have you got to lose except meaningless moments?
- Consider the great TV ad "brought to you by Kleenex" where a guy sits on a couch at a busy intersection and waits. People walk by, sit down, and pour their hearts out. He listens. No fix-its. No advice. No judgments. Just transparency and radical presence.

"What is apt to happen if you don't create conversations of consequence are conversations of default that are not nourishing, inspiring or forward-moving. These days ahead are great opportunities for light-bearing. Share what has inspired you. Take home some good news stories. Feed the hearts and minds of those you love."

—Jan Phillips

The Guest House

This being human is a guest house.
Every morning a new arrival.
A joy, a depression, a meanness, some momentary awareness
comes as an unexpected visitor.
Welcome and entertain them all!
Even if they're a crowd of sorrows,
who violently sweep your house empty of its furniture,
still treat each guest honorably.
He may be clearing you out for some new delight.
The dark thought, the shame, the malice,
meet them at the door laughing, and invite them in.
Be grateful for whoever comes,
because each has been sent as a guide from beyond.

—Mewlana Jalaluddin Rumi, translation by Coleman Barks

MAKE IT YOUR OWN

1. Ask someone to join you in this experiment called courageous conversation. Listen to each other until each feels really empty having said *what wants to be said.*

2. Stretch your comfort zone beyond a spouse or good friend. Invite an unknown human to this adventure! Running out of what to say? Just stay there, more will bubble up. Do it often. You are in training! You are learning to live life full out!

3. Imagine yourself as a "tuning fork." The cleaner you are, the truer your sound. Other humans can help you empty and re-tune! Ask for it and give it—that's edge work.

4. Is this a striptease moment for you? Are there relationships that just don't nourish either of you anymore? You might say to yourself in meditation: "I release____________________ without judgment of myself or _______________. I do this now because it is time."

Consider the Mother Code

"The world is lonely for the comfort of the hips and breasts of women."

—Clarissa Pinkola Estes

A biological mother I am not, but a carrier of mothering energy I am. I never quite knew what that meant until I encountered a woman who spoke little, but touched a lot, using her ample body and soul-piercing eyes to reach beyond people's defenses and physical wariness. She is Amache, a spiritual mother of India.

Amache has hugged to her breasts millions of people who wait for hours in long lines for the experience. Many years ago, I went to sit with Amache in Santa Fe, New Mexico. The tent was packed. People sat on rugs that covered the ground, a miasma of sweet incense filled the air, and baskets of flowers in eye-popping colors lit the space. Indian men playing serpentine music sensually drew us into the present moment. Amache sat cross-legged on her cushion at the front, beaming white teeth in an ecstatic smile.

One by one people made their way to the front, crouching down and giving themselves over to the experience of being hugged—I mean really hugged—to Amache's bosom: each pressed in a loving crush, their faces held firmly in her hands, her eyes looking into their eyes, laughing with a joy we each wanted to capture for ourselves.

I noticed a man waiting in line, suited up in pants, white shirt, and tie loosened at the neck. He looked haggard, work-worn from the day, I imagine. When his turn came, Amache "managed" his body into a position close to the center of her heart, her strong brown hands pressing him deeply to her. Unexpectedly, he gave over to deep wailing sobs, dissolving into a small boy being comforted at his mother's breast, allowing whatever tension and grief to resolve in her embrace. I sat there, tears welling up, saying to myself: *This is real mothering. This is beyond anything I have ever experienced. This is the great mother energy that lives in us. I want this. I want to open myself to loving as deliberately and sensually. I too want to comfort LIFE in this way.*

Amache modeled a primal body-centered power, a kind of *mother code*, that comforts and transforms without words, soothing the internal world of humans with the "there- there" experience that we never outgrow, no matter our age—we who are so hungry "for the comfort of the hips and breasts of women."

In contrast, I find our Western idea of mothering so limited and "baby-bound," when in fact the urge to nourish and protect life is a much greater force of Nature that helps us to know who we really are as female. It provides a fierceness of purpose that brings us back to our wildness, to our true nature at play in the natural order rather than the human order of things.

Some of us have been biological mothers and some have not. Either way, our unequivocal wiring to nurture, to tend life, is the source of the creative impulse within us.

Perhaps it is a new spiritual frontier in midlife to own this greater force of mothering in the world. To bond together in a fierce courage that makes us incapable of any action or of supporting any action that does not nourish, sustain, and defend life in all its forms.

How much of female discontent, depression, and confusion comes from going against our very nature as creators rather than destroyers. If we carry this greater mothering "code" far beyond the biological, as I believe we do, then it is the source of transformative powers available to us through the heart, the belly, the Amache-like body-centered passion in support of all Life.

In this realm, there are no politics, no tribal identities, no borders dictating our care and concern, there is only a cosmic identification, if you will, with the greater destiny of the feminine energy to shift human culture toward connection.

MAKE IT YOUR OWN

1. What is your relationship to touch and affection? Is it easy or tentative? Either way, you thrive through touch and affection. How can you expand into touching and being touched by life?

2. Imagine yourself as an "Amache," deeply embracing others with clear intention. How does it feel? What does it evoke in you?

3. Are you willing to open to this aspect of your nature as great mother energy? Are you willing to practice this with others as a way to open up your own life?

4. What changes would you need to make in your life if this fierceness for nurturing life became a guiding principle?

The Ladybugs Cometh: Reading the Waters

Who has not experienced the almost unrelenting urge **to make it happen, to do it, to get out there and make your mark?**

To my sensibilities, this "thrust and parry" attitude toward taking action does not match up with woman's deepest nature, although most of us have been out there with the best of them practicing just that.

In midlife, the wisdom of the ladybug arrives to teach a way perfectly suited to changing our pace, our rhythm: adopting a dance that moves with life rather than assaulting it!

In the movie *Under the Tuscan Sun*, one of the characters listens to the main character lament that following a divorce and a move to romantic Tuscany, her new life is not taking shape fast enough or to her liking. The friend, frustrated with the main character's frustration, tells her that as a child she would relentlessly and unsuccessfully "rake through the field grasses" in search of ladybugs. Finally, she would be so tired and frustrated by not finding them that she would eventually just collapse in the grass and fall asleep... When she would awake, there would be ladybugs crawling all over her!

Learning to "read the waters" in your life, knowing when to vigorously pursue something and when to "fall asleep in the grass" and just let it happen, is not only a huge shift in perspective, but also a remarkable way to create the magical experience of dancing *with* life rather than engineering it!

Your deepest female self knows such a rhythm. It knows that life is meant to flow and that the ladybugs are meant to show up. It is a further practice in trust. It is a further practice in living an option-filled life created by an option-filled state of mind, fluid and flexible. This is the stuff of peace and ease, an inner climate that fully and completely supports the bubbling up of joy!

If not now, when?

MAKE IT YOUR OWN

1. Identify an aspect of your life where you are "in angst and frustration" to make something happen that you think you want.
2. Are you clear about this thing you want? Can you feel it? Taste it? See it? Does your body say a big YES when you think about it? No reservations?
3. If you had this experience, person, place, or thing, how would you feel?
4. Are you willing to know it can be yours?
5. Your work is done. Now, go lie in the grass and trust it is on its way.

I Will Meet You at the Wailing Wall: Cultivating a Moist Heart

"Sister, you have need of a Sister friend because you need to weep and you need someone to watch you while you weep!"

—Maya Angelou

The Secret Life of Bees by Sue Monk Kidd is a personal favorite; it is a story showing the ways of women creating a culture of care.

In the story, the character May has a very thin emotional membrane between her experience of the world and the pain that is so much a part of it. She feels cruelty and injustice too deeply to be able to endure it. Among her sisters, the standard admonition is: "Don't tell May, it will upset her!"

May's sisters come up with a creative way to help her endure. In the backyard, they build a rock wall, a wailing wall of sorts, a place where May can go to write her pain on small sheets of paper and then tuck the sorrow safely away into the wall. This gives her a measure of relief and control: a way to live with a too-open heart.

A Native American woman once told me that it is imperative that we *do* cultivate a "moist" heart. Similarly, Lily Tomlin remarked that the most radical gift we can give at this time in our world is tenderness. To cultivate a moist heart and its expression of tenderness, one must stay alive to *feeling!* One must not be incapacitated by pain, and yet, one must beware of filters that so numb us that we lose our deep capacity to know truths through our hearts.

May releases her pain in the stones, Lily suggests the practice of tenderness, and Native American wisdom reminds us to be intentionally moist-hearted.

No effective mothering of self or other happens without a heart that can *feel*, a heart that can be fierce and tender at one and the same time. Stay moist. Beware "numbness" and habits of harm that disconnect and separate you from feeling the juice.

Midlife is a "take stock" time—a time to give over to what is real, to what matters.

Wail we must, to stay emptied out and lively, but of equal necessity is to celebrate and take note of every personal experience or planetary happening that nourishes. If we miss either circumstance, we are diminished; life then only happens around us, not through us in the spirit of connection.

I encourage you to create places in Nature, in backyards, in gardens where personal and planetary happenings can be consciously noted and felt. Places where you take all those "nightly news" moments, often horrendous happenings reported to us casually, and honor them: these experiences of animals, fellow humans, and the elemental Earth. It is a way of practicing connection, kinship with the whole of us.

We do this as one way to cultivate our moist hearts. We do this to remain whole and available, tender and awake.

MAKE IT YOUR OWN

1. Gather your friends. Create a space, a shrine, a wall, a sculpture upon which to "spend" your feelings and evoke your tenderness. Make it fun, colorful—a place to tuck your private thoughts, add bits of imagery, candles.

2. Ritual and ceremony are so important to keep us grounded and connected inside and out. Take time with others to mark both painful as well as celebratory events going on here on Earth, our mutual home!

3. It is all about "staying current with the current of life" and continuously releasing in order to stay clean and clear and *available,* over and over again. We wail. We cry. We laugh. All for the health and life of it!

"Come to the table. Come to the feast. We are preparing a place for you.
Take what you need. There's all that you need.
We are preparing a place for you."

—Anonymous

24 Travel Keeps You Macro

"One doesn't discover new lands without consenting to lose sight of shore for a very long time."

—Andre Gide

I am a traveler. I have even joked that I have "suitcases for feet." It is a necessity for me because "travel keeps me macro," a phrase I picked up from a friend describing how she gives herself one international trip a year because it is food to her; she must have it.

Taking borderless broad literally, I passionately believe in travel as a necessity to remain moist-hearted, aware, and in love with life in all its cultural colors.

I traveled to Morocco for a sacred music festival. A land as different from my own as could possibly be, it was a place where the clothing, the food, the music, the landscape, and everyday life was a sensual banquet. Every afternoon and evening, I attended a sacred music event. Musicians and singers come together from all over the world, not so much to entertain, but to share a timeless connection to the divine as they experience it.

Under the night sky in an outdoor amphitheater, I listened to Greek priests chant to the Virgin Mary while across the same stage dervishes whirled and Sufis chanted to Miriam, the Virgin Mary so named in the Quran. I listened to New Orleans black gospel intermingled with the sacred from Asia. Night after night, the borders of religion blurred as performers blended their spiritual natures with one another and the international audience. I felt very "macro."

One afternoon, walking around a plaza in Fes, I joined hundreds of Moroccans gathered for a concert. Totally caught up in the music of a middle-aged Arabic woman and the exotic sounds of her band, I could not stop myself from joining in, swaying, arms waving as I vocalized to the sounds.

Suffice it to say, women do not sway or sing with abandon in public in Morocco, but there I was unself-consciously doing just that. I noticed women turning around and looking at me. I smiled. They smiled and giggled sheepishly. I was a foreigner, after all, and they indulged me.

I noticed a young Moroccan woman covered from head to toe looking at me from out of the crowd. She had a stroller in front of her and another young woman with her. Our eyes met. I was continuing to smile, out of my head with gratitude for this experience. All of sudden, she came rushing over to me, took a hold of my shoulders, looked deeply into my eyes, and then hugged me with the ferocity of a long-lost sister. Twice she repeated this gesture. I hugged back with the same intensity of feeling. We laughed, tears welling up, and then... she went back to her baby and friend.

I came across the world for that moment. I believe she saw my love and appreciation for her culture and it moved her. I believe she vicariously delighted in a woman being able to express emotion in public and it moved her. I was moved by her warmth and spontaneous display of joy and love without borders.

Too soon, it was time to leave Morocco. I was in tears at the airport. Going through security, I had to show my passport to a soldier holding a machine gun at the last door before getting on the plane. Without thinking, I grabbed his sleeve, not even registering that I might get myself shot. I just looked up at him, with tears in my eyes, and said: "I love your country and I thank you for letting me visit." He looked shocked for a moment and then with ***tears in his eyes*** said: "You are a nice lady."

I offer this to you as an incentive to go, risk, travel, be macro, be nourished, and share the banquet of this magnificent world! There can never be too much sharing, too much feeling, too much appreciation and gratitude shown to one another to cultivate a moist heart!

MAKE IT YOUR OWN

I believe we are called to certain places. We have a fascination with a location or country. There is something there for us to discover or to remember from a past lifetime (if you so believe) or to open us up in some way.

1. Tack a world map onto the wall, and in a very relaxed and open attitude, scan it. Let your eyes move over the different areas. Pay attention to your body sensations. You will feel a recognition, excitement, or interest when you see certain places.

2. Pay attention to images from other cultures or landscapes that catch your eye. Make a collage of them and see what it is telling you about your own journeys.

3. Trust it. Go macro!

Leaving the Coliseum

This piece was inspired by the midterm elections in 2010 because I was so angry at the two-party oppositional structure of our government. A government suffering from the *paralysis of polarities* due to some wacky belief that government is a game of football in which "teams," the two bodies of Congress, will somehow miraculously be servants of the people, able to make wise decisions for the good of all through the process of offensive and defensive posturing. It functions as a contemporary *arena* mimicking the Roman gladiators, suited up in armor, entering the coliseum each day to bludgeon each other, winner take all, except there never is a winner, just paralysis.

Oppositional anything is a model of war. It reflects a primitive belief that we can somehow come to agreement or "peace" by going to war. We do it daily within ourselves: at war with our bodies, at war with our ideas about "getting ahead," at war with our thoughts about how it should be or we should be or they should be. Warring only creates paralysis, ruts of stuckness that siphon off our life force, the very exuberance that makes life *flow* and be meaningful, fun, and creative.

Warring is motivated by fears—unexamined fears, cultural fears, leftover waste from millennia of believing war works to "settle things."

I am only concerned with inner wars, my own and yours, because that is where you lose the inner resolve to create the life you want. You lose the resolve to be powerful movers of energy on the planet, tenders of life!

Edge women do not wage war. It is a waste of why you are here and what you are here to do. Believe it. Create a life that rejects oppositional thinking and acting at every turn. Stay clear of your inner gladiator. Opposition confines your soul!

MAKE IT YOUR OWN

1. Where in your life are you "at war"? With yourself? Your body? Your thoughts? Others?

2. You can take off the armor and leave the coliseum. Create a visualization in your imagination. You are standing in the middle of the coliseum, looking up at the crowds. You get a surging realization that you are tired of being a participant in the "war world view" you were trained to have. Imagine taking off your helmet and your breastplate, throwing down your sword, and walking out across the coliseum as the hushed crowd looks on in shock. You feel yourself lightening up, breathing deeper, feeling a freedom you have never had. You leave the coliseum. You have left any and all wars wherever they may be, within and without.

3. How will this change your life? What changes in choices and decisions will this make in your life?

4. Treat it now as a practice. Every day remind yourself: "I have left the coliseum," and apply it to whatever arises.

Match Your Nature with *Nature*

"Now and again, it is necessary to schedule yourself among deep mountains and hidden valleys to restore your link to the source of life. Breathe in and let yourself soar to the ends of the universe, breathe out and let the cosmos back inside. Next, breathe up all the fecundity and vibrancy of the earth with that of your own, becoming the breath of life itself."

—Morihei Ueshiba Osensei

Consider yourself to be elephant, whale, bear, buffalo, or great ape, sharing energies with these remarkably massive creatures. The large beings on our planet "hold" the earth —their energy is deliberate, big, and compelling. They command a respect from us and a sense of their weighty dominion here. This may be your tribe. This is often the tribe of larger women, if they will recognize it and be peaceful!

No one ever says: "That elephant is too fat! That whale should lose weight!"

Consider that you have friends who are bird, rabbit, and fox, sharing energies with the fleet of foot, the small, wily, and quick. No one ever says: "That hummingbird should slow down!"

We all have our tribes beyond the human! It is truly absurd to think that humans do not mimic nature in our bodily configurations and energetic dispositions. Among my friends, I know gazelles and squirrels as well as whales and elephants, hearts beating with rhythms that ONE and ALL match the heartbeat of the Universe.

When we see differences in our glorious human expression and obsessively try to turn ourselves into Barbie-doll-like clones, we diminish who we are as energetic beings. We breed only one-dimensional women who are often secretly longing to be free of their plastic image—blonde, size 0-2, and eternally hungry to feel full. Give it up!

There is a purpose to the energetic packages we come in: each has a purpose beyond our current understanding.

"Make your heartbeat match the beat of the Universe,
match your nature with Nature."

—Joseph Campbell

MAKE IT YOUR OWN

1. Look to Nature. Find beings whose energy is like your own. Find beings whose size or shape is like your own. Find beings for which you feel a special kinship. Ask why.
2. Invite these beings into your life. Gather images. Join with them, heartbeat to heartbeat. They are your allies.
3. Paint them. Sculpt them. Make songs or poems about them. Dance them. Plant a garden in their honor.
4. Include them in your inner family, soul friend to soul friend. You need their care and protection, and they need yours.
5. There are so many opportunities to take vows of fidelity with more than one other being. **Fall in love with the planet, and romance those beings with which you feel a deep connection!**

Clap Your Hands If You Believe in Fairies

There are mammals that are called crepuscular because they prefer to wander at twilight times, meaning dawn and dusk. I am such a mammal, feeling more in myself at transition times when dawn is giving way to day or dusk is giving way to night. I share this with cats, dogs, rabbits, mice, and wombats, to name just a few fellow crepusculars! I bring this up because this is one of those things that we don't think much about. Things that are hidden from us in our everyday consciousness, sort of like fairies!

There are many things we do not think about, like how many people are sleeping around the globe when we are awake or how many people are awake when we are sleeping or that millions of us unfold prayer rugs and prostrate ourselves in prayer five times a day. We might not realize either that every sunrise and sunset deserves a standing ovation, and somewhere in the world, someone is doing just that.

And then there are other important things like knowing that bubbles love early morning moisture and never more than a slight breeze. That blowing bubbles is a perfect opportunity to send them on an adventure, freed from their liquid existence, and a way for you to meditate on the lightness of being...

That everyday people can transform into Holy Fools who delight and awaken their fellow humans by choosing to "see" differently and share that "seeing." One such Holy Fool, Joseph Martin, encourages us to liberate ice cubes by taking them back to a lake or pond and returning them to their source. He suggests we learn to really listen, and when we have learned, we will hear the sound of clouds bumping into each other and leaves changing color and people changing their minds.

Which brings me to fairies... If you recall, Peter Pan's Tinkerbell was dying, and the only way to save her, to recharge her life force, was for all children everywhere to clap madly, loudly, and exuberantly, believing with all their might in fairies. Tinkerbell was saved, and now it is a well- known fact that fairies come alive everywhere when we clap and believe!

I think these kinds of awareness are important. They take our thinking out of the grooves and over the edge.

One does not just wake up one day having a happy life. One must do a series of happy and exuberant things that then, when we are not looking, turn into a happy life—things like becoming crepuscular for a time and noticing what happens and how we feel at these rarified times of the day.

"There is great power in joining with others in raucous celebration."
—Morgana Morgaine

MAKE IT YOUR OWN

1. Practice listening to things you believe have no sound.
2. Mark certain times of the day with your own version of holiness. Pause and connect to whatever takes you beyond borders and to the edge places within yourself. Bring a prayer rug, if it helps you remember.
3. Get a group and give standing ovations to each other, the stars, the full moon, and the new moon and clap yourself silly for the fairies. Get out of your "too serious" self.
4. The point is to move into wonder and glee, raise your vibration, and simply feel more alive, wildly happy, and available to life!

28

It's a Wrap & That Makes You the Rainmaker!

A village is in drought conditions. The land is barren. People are depressed and angry. Nothing grows or replenishes itself. The village council calls for a prayer vigil. First, the Catholics make procession, chanting and burning incense. Next the Protestants make procession, quoting biblical passages. Finally, the Buddhists make procession, with bells and prayer wheels. Nothing happens. Nothing helps. A villager suggests a rainmaker from an adjoining country. The council decides to send for her. An old wizened woman arrives. She tells the people that she needs a small house in which to be alone. The house is provided. Two days pass. Three days pass. The villagers are impatient and wonder what she is doing. On the fourth morning, the wind begins to blow and the sky clouds over. Soon it is raining cats and dogs! The woman comes out, and the villagers, overjoyed, surround her. "What did you do? What did you do?" they ask. The woman replies: "I come from a country where we live in balance. When I arrived in your village, I could feel that everything here was out of order. I felt that disorder within myself. I had to go inside and find balance again, and then...of course, the rains came!"

To be effective, you strive for balance within yourself. If you are unsure of your center, your own inner home, then you waste tremendous energy in self-doubt. You do things like accept jobs, create relationships, and make choices and decisions that are "out of order" with who you really are.

Imagine being able to describe yourself as clearly and succinctly as author Deirdre Green described the great mystic, Theresa of Avila:

"At 50,
She left her spiritual adolescence behind her;
Found the purpose of her life,
Scope of her gifts,
And an outlet for her creative energies."

—Deirdre Green, *The Gold in the Crucible:*
Theresa of Avila & the Western Mystical Tradition

This book, *Borderless Broads,* is an act of power for me. It is also my effort to *whip you into a frenzy for reenvisioning your midlife!* I am urging you to make your own act of power: to fully step into a life of your creating, to show up, and to have the courage to let go of aspects of your training that hold you back from your own balance and from interpreting your own world, your inner and outer home.

Becoming borderless means redefining your boundaries, not by what your culture defines as appropriate, but by what supports and encourages your expression in the world. This takes self-reflection. It takes Walt Whitman's admonition to: "Re-examine all that you have been told...dismiss that which insults your soul."

There are many "directives" for coming into balance in your life. Elizabeth Gilbert says: "eat, pray, love." The monastic Benedictine order offers "Benedict's Rule": pray, work, study. Dolores Leckey suggests an armature upon which to hang your daily life, one that supports the blossoming of your creativity.

Such directives are meant to provide enough structure so that you can benefit from containers that support ***freedom***.

Healthy containers encircle your energy and provide enough order to your life so that consistent focus becomes possible. They offer the supportive opportunity to maintain a certain direction that allows you to deepen, to quiet, and to become a woman of soul-guided resolve! You can then devote yourself to the fullest fruit of your unique creative expression while distraction, depletion of energy, and the scattering of one's life force diminishes. You feel more purposeful and energetic, rather than fatigued and aimless.

Directives are not prisons, they are powerhouses! They allow you to relax into rhythmic cycles of activity that nourish you and the individuals of your pod, if you choose a more communal lifestyle, that is. They provide a space where big dreams, great work (the magnum opus), and focused lives can materialize; they give us the opportunity to become rainmakers!

I encourage every midlife woman who resonates with this book to turn in the direction of awake, purposeful living and to take her self-expression in this third destiny time of life to heart and to action.

It took me a long time to realize that intentional self-chosen containment is the direct path to freedom and incredible creative output. Do I know this is true because I have fully realized this vision? No! But I know it to be true, call it a memory from another time or a direct transmission from the collective mind. It does not matter. It is truth. It is timely, and its time is now.

MAKE IT YOUR OWN

1. What resonates most with you in this book? Use it to further your own delight in living.
2. Get a group. Read the book. Have each woman take a part that spoke most to her and share with the group.
3. Out of this sharing comes magic, and magic creates borderless broads and edge women able to make copious rain in their own lives and for the good of the whole on our Earth!
4. What are your next steps? I am eager to know! (Contact me at Morgana@MorganaMorgaine.com.)

Magic for Midlife Mystics, Mavericks, and Mavens: "Tag, You're It!"

Multiple identities are fun. They expand who we are and inspire and motivate us to give voice to all the experiences that have shaped us. Consider the mystic, the maverick, and the maven. Use them to expand your sense of who you are. Use them to map out your adventure. This is a game of tag, and now, you are it!

As a Midlife Mystic, you are enlivened by spiritual passion, understanding what it is to be swept away by the indefinable, the ineffable. The possibility of deep communion with unseen worlds delights you. You speak the language of surrender. You are an open vessel continually seeking and finding the divine in all things. You practice presence, which allows you to attend to life's details moment by moment. (Inspired by Angi Sullins, Duirweigh Studios, and my own musings!)

As a Midlife Maverick, you are unbranded, untamed—a borderless broad. You draw no distinction between the nature around you and that within. You define and live your own truth, speaking through your deepest wild self. (Same inspirations as above.)

As a Midlife Maven, you are defined as an enthusiast carrying the wise woman legacy, which says: Live Life Full Out!

I end with a few "bits of wisdom" that, as I came upon them in my own life, sent me madly running to others, exclaiming: "Listen to this. This is truth; I just *know* it! This came from some kind of cosmic library. You've just got to let this in!"

I offer them to you who aspire to define yourselves as borderless broads, edge women extraordinaire. Believers that magic is always afoot!

"To play a useful role in the great divine plan, you must be able to use your own person, like an obedient instrument, in front of the public. You must be able, in front of groups of other people, to animate your talents and abilities with your spiritual forces, raise them to a climax of brilliance in such a way that you manifest your spirit in the highest degree through your person, through the posture of your body, through the movements of your hands, through the glance of your eyes and through the persuasive power of your speech, all so that you carry people upward with you to a higher spiritual level."

—Elisabeth Haich, *Initiation*

"When you put yourself out into the world and don't receive the results you think you deserve, it's not necessarily because your work is substandard or because you're doing something wrong. You must keep going, keep walking, taking the steps that come from the deepest impulses. What makes people notice you and your work is power, and you have not built up enough of it. ***Power*** *accumulates by consistently using the talents you were given, from doing what you love repeatedly in the world. Be creative every day. Be the artist and do the artwork. Don't siphon energy into other activities and people. Be convincing.*

You must saturate your energy field with who and what you are!"

—Penney Peirce, *The Intuitive Way*

"When the conversation with your deepest nature becomes your guidance system, then the real joy begins..."

—Morgana Morgaine

"Every moment
A voice
Out of this world
Calls on our soul
To wake up and rise

This soul of ours
Is like a flame
With more smoke than light
Blackening our vision
Letting no light through

Lessen the smoke and
More light brightens your house
The house you dwell in now
And the abode
You'll eventually move to

Now my precious soul
How long are you going to
Waste yourself
In this wandering journey
Can't you hear the voice

Can't you use your swifter wings
And answer the call?"

—Rumi, "Fountain of Fire," *Nader Khalili*

Tag, you're it.

Borderless Broads, it's now all yours to *Make It Your Own*...

Morgana Morgaine offers:

- **Training workshops designed for women in midlife seeking to live a more collective lifestyle**, what she calls "pod living." She advocates lifestyle choices that offer the right balance of supportive structure and individual sovereignty to nurture women who seek to deepen spiritually, to explode into creative expression, and to thrive!

  Her workshops invite women to consider "Beguine-thinking," taking a journey back to 13th century Europe to be inspired by a group of women who successfully lived and worked in creative collectives! (E-mail her at Morgana@MorganaMorgaine.com.)

- **Keynotes and workshops** on "Living Your Life through the Lens of Laughter" and "Turning Working Professionals into Healthy Humorists, One Red Nose at a Time!" **Laughter and Play are essential elements for living a "higher octave" life.** These events are offered to any human eager to enjoy the "art of play"! (See www.HumorIsHealthy.com for more information.)

- **Her e-book, "Turn Depression into Expression, 5 Ways to *Move* You."** DOWNLOAD the book from www.MorganaMorgaine.com. **Depression of any kind stops you in your tracks and prevents you from living life full out**! It is an epidemic these days.

- **Individual and group coaching** for individuals interested in repurposing their life's journey for inner peace and outer success! (See www.MorganaMorgaine.com for more information.)

Morgana@MorganaMorgaine.com

www.MorganaMorgaine.com

www.HumorIsHealthy.com